a memory of elephants

christian reynolds

ISBN: 0-578-42261-1
ISBN-13: 978-0-578-42261-9

for Jason and Danny

a special thanks to my mom for her editing prowess and suggestions; to my dad for his continuous support; to family and friends who lent me their eyes and ears; and to my wife, Courtney, who has endured my "will you read this?" for twenty years contents

the elephant

i hear his trumpet roars in the night
i feel the tread of his heavy feet

roaming the planes of a lonely void
he is a ghost in a formless frame

and then his grey shape grows into lines
see tone and mood start to form his face

his ears are words in the mindful wind
his eyes are rhymes the light can't escape

bent spear-like tusks that refuse to harm
his sweeping trunk is a writer's arm

look now emerging from endless dark
he leaves my mind to peruse the light

and then he lowers his trunk and smiles
in strict rhythm it sways left to right

and spryly plunges onto the page
now he has found his watering place

consciousness flows (i)

consciousness flows
consciousness flows
consciousness flows

from line to line
from rhyme to rhyme
from time to time

this schematic
it's not static
fancy fabric

of thoughts that grow
how needles sew
these thoughts. you know

lines deliver
like a river
each a sliver

it is magic
enigmatic
they're not static

i was
once the drink in an aged king's cup
the wine in some emperor's flask
the water that flows and follows
the odd track of this human cask

i was
sweeping snow on arctic tundra
amplified Pacific tides
tears of Adam and sweat of Eve
drops of south Saharan sky

i was
forged and diffused through space
the last breath of a dying star
sifted through sands and sterilized
into ancient rivers afar

i am
the forgotten names and places
of who and what came before me
water i was   water i am
and water is what

i will be

departure

i saw some geese take wing today
beneath a lifeless stubborn grey
sky that warned
of a creeping storm
and i wished those geese would get away

something simmers within their blood
whether it be instinct or mood
i do not know
still i watched them go
and disappear from where i stood

south they flew to find new fame
to share their song with other game
i am told
they leave the cold
only to return again the same

soon a current of warmth will bring
back those creatures of familiar wing
this i hold true
but what will i do
if those birds do not return in spring?

i have been where the mind races the heart
that rapid rhythm of a constant thought
at night i gaze inward to find my art

restless eyes that beat beat inches apart
and yet my dreams remain a dream uncaught
i have been where the mind races the heart

the yawned-out years i have strained to outsmart
my own thoughts and ideas i have fought
at night to gaze inward to tame my art

so sleep will wait while closed eyes are the darts
aiming for those perfections i have sought
i have been where the mind races the heart

and from this slow sleeplessness i will start
untangling the twines of truth i was taught
at night i gaze inward to hone my art

restless eyes that beat beat inches apart
that rapid rhythm of a constant thought
i have been where the mind races the heart
at night i gaze inward and *is* my art

what poetry does not do

it doesn't drift
like unfounded rumors
in dusty social circles

or share shameless
political politeness
on Baltic Avenue purple

nor does it do toasts
with vodka villanelles
with strangers at sea

mostly it just sits in my stomach
as silent lines
flexing to be free

standing in the rain a circus
waits to board a tireless train
it gathers to collect its things
a couple of uncolored clowns
(just humans really)
neither smile nor frown
as they push the pachyderms
up a sodden ramp
its damp slope daunting
to the oldest elephant
who watches this parade
as his grey leather fades
and fights the cold and weary weather

soon he is pulled and persuaded
(a thousand towns from feeling elated)
up and up his destiny's ramp
and he wonders what would be better
being wetter in New Jersey or the Sahara
his tusks were not made
for trains or for trade
to be a prisoner here or hunted there
he guesses then
that it's all about the same

an unguided guider

        i am being guided
          by an unguided guider
            who lights the way
              without a light
                and just when i think
                  it's all in my head
                    he speaks his mind
                  out of spite

or just a motion

                      we are fluid
                        pieces
                        in a
                    time puzzle
                    unsolvable
                    and forever
                          flowing
                    is the motion
                    not canaled
                    or steered?
                  we are cursed
                    in our
                  never knowing

the turtle

the night above us
is the dark underbelly
of a great turtle

out of ancient myths
she is goddess of the wise
and the most fertile

she is the mother
of the moon the whole cosmos
and time eternal

and then there is Zeus
who crawls not across the sky
but hides immortal

from a heavenly
place he waits shrouded in clouds
lightning to hurtle

so given the choice
(the metaphor or the god?)
i'd take the turtle

headlines six/four/fifteen

watch the drunken wobble
of Pluto's smaller moon
the Shabab's deadly attacks
leave a void in Kenya's schools

and Seinfeld killed off Susan
(actress impossible to work with)
Jurassic Park's huge plot hole
that you might've missed

and this is what the end looks like
for Rafael Nadal
to boost its sales Taco Bell
will serve us alcohol

and FIFA paid off Ireland
to not protest a game
Putin threatens to battle
the sanctions for Ukraine

so these were the headlines
such a motley mix to swallow
too much news is too much
i no longer choose to follow

for on that day six/four/fifteen
the news was set to nobble
this is what the end looks like
watch the drunken wobble

to supernova

a night sky
   over the ocean
      gust of light
       a strange sun's motion
       abstract allusion
       starburst confusion

      from steadiness
         to supernova
            a titanic transition
             the creative combustion
             is the wand-wave
             of magicians

            when a poem
               is formed from
                a single notion
                 my mind becomes
                 a celestial body
                 explosion

complicated stone

(we are
complicated
stone
the illusion
of free will
and thought
each
to each
we are not
our own
contrary
to what
we were
taught)

someday
i would
love to find
what all
philosophers
fathom
whether
the
atom
moves
the mind
or the mind
the

                              atom

a matter of light and death

we know now
light is a particle
and a wave
and we can't match
or break its speed
(so they say)
but light
is simple enough
and to my delight
(and my decay)
the world is full of it

so when i
(so limited)
finally move on
as a wave or particle
(or glossy gluon)
i will evaporate
commensurate
with its effect
and help make visible
the moon
and the stars

and all of the sunsets

running

i run
through out
the streets
not to
compete
but to
complete
a race
meant just
for me

the streets
they are
my mind
and i
unwind
most of
the time
the paths
no one
can see

i run
along
with hope
up the
steep slope
just to
invoke
the words
of what
will be

i run
where no
one can
to plot
the plan
to un-
derstand
this need
to be
so free

i leap
into
the night
not as
a flight
but to
ignite
the light
inside
of me

there is
so much
to say
maybe
one day
i can   stop
                         running!

running
running
running
i run
away

17

the inaccuracy of memory

i was given everything i needed to see
cloud
white
sky
blue
and
ocean
green
i
squeezed
them
on
a
palette
and
then
one
two
three
i
closed
my
eyes
and tried to paint the sky reflected in the sea

it's like the fourth of July in here

sometimes
i find myself
growing conscious
in the strangest
of places

last time
i was in a Target
flanked by waxy apples
and impossibly
cold beer

an English woman
with
unruly children
a wild collage
of Wrangler blue jeans

knocked into
a case of Heinz ketchup
scattering red flecks
on the white floor
and i thought

it's like the fourth of July in here

consciousness flows (ii)

from time to time
consciousness flows
like a river
how needles sew
fancy fabric
it's not static

from line to line
consciousness flows
each a sliver
of thoughts that grow
this schematic
enigmatic

from rhyme to rhyme
consciousness flows
lines deliver
these thoughts. you know
they're not static
it is magic

a memory of elephants (i)

3

under an orange
awning of dawn
the grey pachyderms
proceed across the prairie
swaying trunks to the scent
of siblings headed towards
peaceful waters

2

alone she blinks
and fans her ears
in the Samburu sun
the flies crawl on her
dry belly

1

endangered Khadija
recalls her family
before she is shot
from behind
in the
head

funny how tusks are free
    to roam

leave their lifeless bodies
    like souls

get hacked into hardware for
    a home

incisors sized into tiny
    white bowls

or finger rings, vases, or handles
    for knives

billiard balls, buttons, or Scottish
    bagpipes

two tusks separated by space
    and time

pulled from the prairie when in
    their prime

they leave their lifeless bodies
    like souls

funny how tusks are free
    to roam

blues song

you tiptoe round my heart
but you're never steppin' in

there's room for this to start
so let's let this love begin

you're climbin' up my charts
oh this line we walk is thin

so keep tiptoein' round my heart
and decide if you're steppin' in

but the rules they fall apart
feel i'm never goin' to win

'cause your voice is like a dart
and my heart is made of tin

and i know if you were smart
you'd be seein' my head spin

see i'm tiptoein' round your heart
and it's time to let me in

oh Sylvia

i vanished in our dances
spinning through hidden rooms
those nights of soundless romances
implied little if any doom
my arms embracing
my eyes retracing
your steps line by line
                    i recall i wept

oh Sylvia

i held your spine
as we waltzed
my fingertips entwined
with the thoughts
you permeated into the pages
you were the yellow aged
papyrus i was the pair
                of eyes that watched us

oh Sylvia

i waltzed those evenings away
with your uninhibited mind
as two eyes today
now mix with mine
do they know too
the years of sadness you
were dealt? oh Sylvia
                i know exactly how you felt

of doves

listen to them now
as they come from the clouds
the doves know something
of desire and love
unstressed and resting
on the wire above
each singing and clinging
in their second positions
no need for revisions
neither gloats nor boasts
as they bill and coo
in the morning hue

together they share
a borderless air
finding freedom
with their feathers
among human kingdoms
and human strife
and i think who dares
to understand that in life
it's all about the other?
at least the doves
                   will have
                   each other

when we went walking
over the yellow acres of an apple orchard

summers ago you said you
needed time to process the projected

future. a dark shadow danced among the fruit
trees and we never walked

there again. we never walked again
through that enviously green Eden

even today because of you
the sweetest of red apples taste bitterly blue

the minute

i had
a minute
then i
lost it
and i
don't know
what
to do
like
a leaky
faucet
time is
water
running
through
people
tend to
toss it
the time
i hold
as true
i had
a minute
(just
one minute)
that's all
the time
i had
with you

deconstruction

you
rearranged
the atoms
in my mind
the new queen
of my inquisitor's
quantum

i
want to
disassemble
the molecules
you made
so that you
no longer
haunt them

when next i see her in the clouds

someday (i know the future hides)
when clouds will surge across the sky
white apparitions will emerge
a soundless dirge to analyze

see first there bursts a string of doves
above soft angles slowly shift
into a gift of angels high
gliding along their souls adrift

but then the winds caress the clouds
and morph them into shaggy shapes
a face once known to start a smile
hers was one of endless grace

freely racing out of reach
chasing the pale ball of the moon
my leash-less friend returns to me
to briefly join the afternoon

where have you been my dear old dog?
do you recall this hapless man?
knowing how wind goes on to wind
she fades the clouds disperse again

although i may have years to wait
for now i have what dreams allow
she will be collarless and free
when next i see her in the clouds

love
(and other climates)

your eyes
are melting
glaciers ancient
rivers unfreeze
like faucets
down your
face

i never
knew the
sadness of our
global warming
(i'm warming up
to the chilling
realization)

i am
the heat
trapped in
your oceans
the polluted
w a t e r s
in your
tears

and save them all for you

        if life were filled
          with only so many swallows
           only so many heartbeats
           only so many breaths
            then i would be still
             and eat very little
              and save them all for you

        if life were filled
          with countless swallows
           eternal heartbeats
           and infinite breaths
            then i would be still
             and eat very little
              and save them all for you

breath

i inhale you
and hold you
in my lungs
to keep you
inside of me
but with each

breath

in order for
us to be
i must
exhale you
and set you

free

the petrichor

before the now rain
drenched poplar
leaves lifted and turned
in the turbulent wind
the petrichor
a precursor
the promise of rain
predicted her
before the clouds
painted shadows into
each neat crease
of piercing sun
the petrichor
a precursor
the promise of rain
predicted her
before the now rain
nourished earth
puddles pooled
in Carolina clay
the petrichor
a precursor
the promise of rain
predicted her
before the clouds
crowded the clearly
proud but parched
summer sky
the petrichor
predicted her

           the rainbow
           after the rain

yours

i am yours but not yours
i am free but not free
i am real but not real
i am loved but not loved

i am me but not me
i am healed but not healed
i am here but not here
i am yours but not yours

the murmuration

go to sleep my starling
nestle up and nurture
our distant dreams

for tomorrow you will
rely on the masses
that incumbent murmur

encircle proud peaks
gracefully dodge and drop
in the pixelated clouds

until you pause in that dance
avoid all collisions
and return to nest with me

the sesame ones

i left them
open again
the beige box
of crackers
we
last
picked
from
weeks ago

        they're stale

she says

        no

i say

        that's just their flavor
        the sesame ones
        they just taste
        that way

        oh

she says

        then
        let's not buy
        that kind of cracker
        again
        or
        accidentally
        leave them open

two degrees

there's a two degree difference
between my baby and me

i like seventy-one
and she likes seventy-three

i sweat as she freezes
so what do we do?

we set the temp
on seventy-two

i look at the light how it ages you and me
photographs fade and fast forward
the years made obscure like
reflections on a dappled
sea you no longer
know you i no
longer know
me the light
how it ages
us please
l i g h t
l e t
u s
b
e

a memory of elephants (ii)

Me-Bai and Mae-Yui
stand beneath a sleepy Thai sky

they rub their trunks up
and down each other's side

Me-Bai only three is sold
she will become a tourist ride

Mae-Yui trumpets as they are divided
by a distance too far for cries

Mae-Yui never forgets
she never forgets and waits for Me-Bai

years later she holds her trunk up
against the awakened Thai sky

the scent and a feeling
then fresh memories of Me-Bai

and Me-Bai now seven
too sick to give people rides

is rejoicing and rejoicing
in her mother's only way to say hi

they rub their trunks up
and down each other's side

i will   try to remember   your grand shadow
now only see   the white tin   collectible

you in pictures   paper   things
or clips   of your skin   from the market

the way you   made tough   love and
moved those hips   in captivity   life is fleeting

you died   i think   i know
born to be free   i never got to see   the last white rhino

extinction

Laniakea

Like a dandelion seed dangling in the dark

A cluster of clashing galaxies entrances

Nascent strands dance arms outstretched

Immersed in the immeasurable heavens

And as i search this sonorous star-sung night

Keen perspective ignites in me a spark

Essentially all is just a part of a part of a part

And us? we are a part of it but we are not all of it

a girl in Haiti

she hovered
near the porch
a zombie in a trance
her eyes under the moon
were clouded earths
her dry lips did not dance

but her eyes indeed
spoke something
of hunger and fear
this face knew nothing
of love or grace

i think one of us
gave her plantains
she disappeared
and was forgotten
as we ate our goat
and drank our Prestige

prey and prayer

the   wolf
is a hungry spirit
in the night the
rabbit listens
but stays
out of
sig
ht

the fields

i.

dragonfly dancer of early spring
pilot of nature you hold positions
better than ballet beauties
swiftly diving forward lifting backward
and upside down you are the jester
who by design swims round and round
turn and swing those waxy wings
make this field a stage enraged
in thick shades of green
i sit Indian style and smile and
listen to the soft nano-breeze you spin
as you pass on by
compose the music of this meadow
and try to forget old me
go on with your feeding frenzy
and be free

ii.

green and yellow grasses
grow all around us
an indolent lawn so sleepy
it yawns in the light
but beneath it within it
a storming collage of atoms
must beat and hum and i
fancy them all purposely moving
like tiny creatures controlling
the visible and invisible
and i am unable with my eyes
to locate a single one
but i imagine Blake's tyger
crouching beneath the furious fescue
blowing fire into the equations
asking my inner eye
not for a location
but to realize
                there is no dragonfly

for William S.
(behind the eyes of autism)

i am Theseus
(or Sisyphus perhaps)
in a labyrinth blind
working to find
my way out
or maybe trapped
in Plato's cave
not even knowing
the true face
of the outside world
or a henchman from Hades
roaming a scorched
underworld full of souls
who will not even lift
their eyes to see me
or am i Perseus
instead? and all i need
is the Gorgon's head
to save Cassiopeia's daughter
from old Poseidon's monster
and in an instant
become Andromeda's man
and i think and i think and i think
that you'll never understand
the Minotaur is pursuing me
after all i am the hero in here
and pushing forward
i will always be

after the storm

the violet clouds cling
to invisible shelves
over the city

people peering out
from unwashed windows
at the waning wind

i too peruse from
a low perch i can
feel the street's fierce heat

lift from the pavement
and i swear i see
the city breathing

the night is steaming
people are stirring
and life begins again

the butterflies

to the trees.

to return
in time

backward

fanning

blossoms
reborn

are

Butterflies

an old wind chime

an old wind chime
sways awkwardly silent

in the soft wind
potential and purpose

resting and wanting
an abrupt breeze

to brush by
and melody make

may we all turn
to a quiet corner and

capture the nature
of all things

summer

summer stitches
her sandy hair
through humid August nights

with fireflies
and steamy stars
she embroiders the sky

weaving her way
towards autumn
and all his fading lights

she promises
on falling leaves
that this is not goodbye

a waning moon

who does
  she think
   she is
     with curves
      like that?
        she might
        believe
        she is
        a star
       but i
      hear her
    light is
fading

night, november

        when the moon drips
           and dampens

        the protuberant tips
           of thin trees

        against the canvas strips
           of darkness

        i fondly think of them
           as black pens dipped

        in ash white ink
           ready to write the sky

the heaviness

the windless snow falls
like the inaudible guilt
of a tortured man

the light from windows
passes through curtains, certain
of white-washed remorse

cover everything
and let what's due to its course
(i am one for dreams)

i secretly know
that the snow buries nothing
        but silent screams

of bug and man

on seeing a fly approach the wall
to find a crawly space to crawl
i swatted him at once and watched h
                                    i
                                    m

                                    f
                                    a
                                    l
                                    l .

an ink elephant
(see all the world's a stage)

in the third and fourth ages
i flourished with fortitude and phrasing
poetry and art like a young soldier in spring
marches toward the summer shore in conquest.
here in the seventh age before the last heavy leg
of winter will slip across into the void i find i
am close to a second childishness and of
my faculties i will be fully bereft.
when all the world really is is
a page a stage starring
an ink elephant
and then
that's
all t
ha
t's
le
f
t

fishing for stars

i am fishing
for stars
when at evening
they come on gleaming
like motionless guppy eyes
suspended in an azure sea

i am wishing
to grasp
when at night
i ask quiet questions
and they hang like bright fruit
from a colorless tree

i am fishing
for answers
when at morning
they go on fading
like closing flower buds
in a yellow field

and i am wishing
for stars
when at day
they are dreaming
like sleeping children
who want nothing revealed

in the cosmic dawn
when the universe first yawned
like an awakened child
when miles were not yet miles
and hydrogen and helium swept
into the ever-expanding unswept
single and double electron atoms
most of us can little fathom
attracted mass upon mass until at last
over hundreds of millions of years
gravity condensed the stars like tears
finally igniting those bodies of light
we now see as trivial pinpoints at night
some of them stars and some galaxies
ancient though still visible to me
captured by the slow winking eye
of a telescope turning with the sky
and i am resolved to think
that the original is not extinct
it grows all around me
an aggregated garden of gravity
and light metamorphosed
into everything around us
and all that surrounds us
within us and without us
the gravity and the light

> so absolutely substantial
> so infinitely bright

a memory of elephants (iii)

elephants are
memories

words hiding
in pages

memories are
elephants

too large
for cages

elephants are
memories

sadly facing
a slaughter

memories are
elephants

returning
            to waters

elephants are
memories

heavy thoughts
that remain

memories are
elephants

that cannot
be chained

elephants are
memories

of mothers and
daughters

memories are
elephants

returning
        to waters

Made in the USA
Middletown, DE
14 December 2018